COUNTING
Is for the

Birds

Frank Mazzola, Jr.

Charlesbridge

For Cindy,
my best friend and
bird-watching partner

I wish to thank the following people for their encouragement and support:
my parents, Frank and Gidge, and Juliana.

I also want to thank: Holly and the Massachusetts Audubon Society for lending me the bird mounts;
Betty and Diane for reviewing the manuscript; Mary Ann for her interest in the book; Kelly and Yolanda
for their assistance; Pam for her insight; Jiggs the cat for inspiration;
and Jerry for getting me hooked on children's books.

Published by Charlesbridge Publishing
85 Main Street, Watertown, MA 02472
(617) 926-0329
www.charlesbridge.com

Library of Congress Cataloging-in-Publication Data
Mazzola, Frank.
Counting is for the birds/Frank Mazzola, Jr.
p.   cm.
Includes index.
Summary: As a cat patiently waits, birds from one to twenty land at a feeder.
Includes information about various species and the seeds they eat.
ISBN 0-88106-951-5 (reinforced for library use)
ISBN 0-88106-950-7 (softcover)
1. Counting—Juvenile literature.
2. Birds—Juvenile literature.
[1. Birds. 2. Counting.] I. Title.
QA113.M3925   1997
513.2'11 — dc20   95-25825

Printed in the United States of America
(hc) 10 9 8 7 6 5 4
(sc) 10 9 8 7 6 5 4 3

The illustrations in this book are digital paintings created using a personal computer.
They were painted on-screen using a Wacom tablet and wireless pen. No photography was used.
Final paintings are stored on CD-ROM discs.
The text is set in Adobe Galahad.
Printed and bound by Worzalla Publishing Company, Stevens Point, Wisconsin
Produced and designed by Frank Mazzola, Jr.
This book was printed on recycled paper.

The feeder is still,
    it hangs overhead.
It's morning and time
    for birds to be fed.
This new day begins
    with fog all around.
Be still because there
    are birds to be found.

O

Well hidden below,

    a cat lies in wait.

This cat is greedy,

    his appetite great.

He sees there are **zero**

    birds he can catch,

No birds on the feeder

    for him to snatch.

striped sunflower

black-oiled sunflower

safflower

white millet

The bird feeder in this book contains four kinds of seeds: black-oiled and striped sunflower, safflower, and white millet. This seed medley attracts a wide variety of birds. From black-capped chickadees to blue jays, these birds visit the feeder in search of food.

1   2

Then one chickadee
     grabs on with his feet.
A second floats in,
     her tiny wings beat.
Both birds move quickly,
     so keep them in view.
Count them together
     and you will find two.

These two acrobats are black-capped chickadees. When chickadees feed at a feeder, they take turns. The dominant or stronger bird eats first while the other chickadees wait close by for their turn.

3   4

Three is a titmouse,
   and four is her mate.
These birds are feeding
   at a rapid rate.
These little creatures
   will flee to the trees.
Once they have landed,
   they peck at the seeds.

The tufted titmouse is a relative of the chickadee. Titmice take just one seed at a time and then fly off to the trees. In the safety of the trees, they eat the seed. It is fun to count the number of times chickadees and titmice return to the feeder for more seeds.

5 6

Bird five clutches on
and pecks with his beak.
Number six arrives
and takes a quick peek.
These woodpeckers eat bugs
they find in wood.
They also eat seeds,
which taste really good.

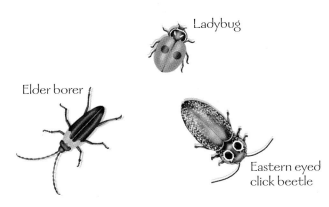

Ladybug

Elder borer

Eastern eyed
click beetle

Downy woodpeckers enjoy eating sunflower seeds, even though insects are
their favorite food. They use their powerful beaks to find bugs in tree trunks,
branches, and bark. Have you ever heard an erratic tapping sound outside?
This may be a downy looking for an insect meal.

7 8

Birds seven and eight
    drop in from up high.
Goldfinches' feathers
    help color the sky.
The number of birds
    grows larger so fast,
The cat still watches
    the birds that fly past.

Like all finches, American goldfinches have conical-shaped beaks that are designed for eating seeds. The conical shape enables the finch to hold on to and crack a seed without using its feet.

Nine is a sparrow,

who dives in with speed.

The tenth comes along

and follows her lead.

Ten birds are feeding,

with plenty to share.

Eating together,

enjoying the fare.

☐ Summer

■ Winter

American tree sparrows are migratory and travel in flocks of up to fifty birds.
In the summer, they live in Alaska and northern Canada. In the fall, they
migrate to southern Canada and to parts of the United States, where they
spend the winter.

11   12

Eleven is red,

he feeds on the ground.

Number twelve swoops in,

not making a sound.

Crouching in silence,

the cat keeps his stare,

While cardinals feed

in front of his lair.

Platform feeder

Hopper feeder

Seeds tossed
on the ground

All three methods
will attract ground–
feeding birds.

Northern cardinals usually feed on the ground and occasionally dine at hanging feeders. During the mating season, the male cardinal brings a seed to the female. If the female accepts the seed, the male and female become mates. This is called mate feeding.

13   14

A famished duo
    is next to arrive.
Thirteen and fourteen,
    these finches will thrive.
Fourteen birds feasting,
    all eating their fill.
Each bird is hungry
    and cracks seeds with skill.

Look, no teeth!

Like all birds, purple finches swallow their food whole because they do not have teeth. Birds have a special muscle in their stomach that grinds the food so that it can be digested. This muscle is called the gizzard.

15   16

Bird fifteen flies by,
        his pal sweeps in, too.
These buntings are colored
        indigo blue.
Sixteen birds eating
        and looking about,
Devouring seeds
        until they run out.

Indigo buntings are shy birds and rarely venture far from the underbrush that protects them. They eat small seeds, weed seeds, and insects. Scattering white millet on the ground near the underbrush may lure them out into view.

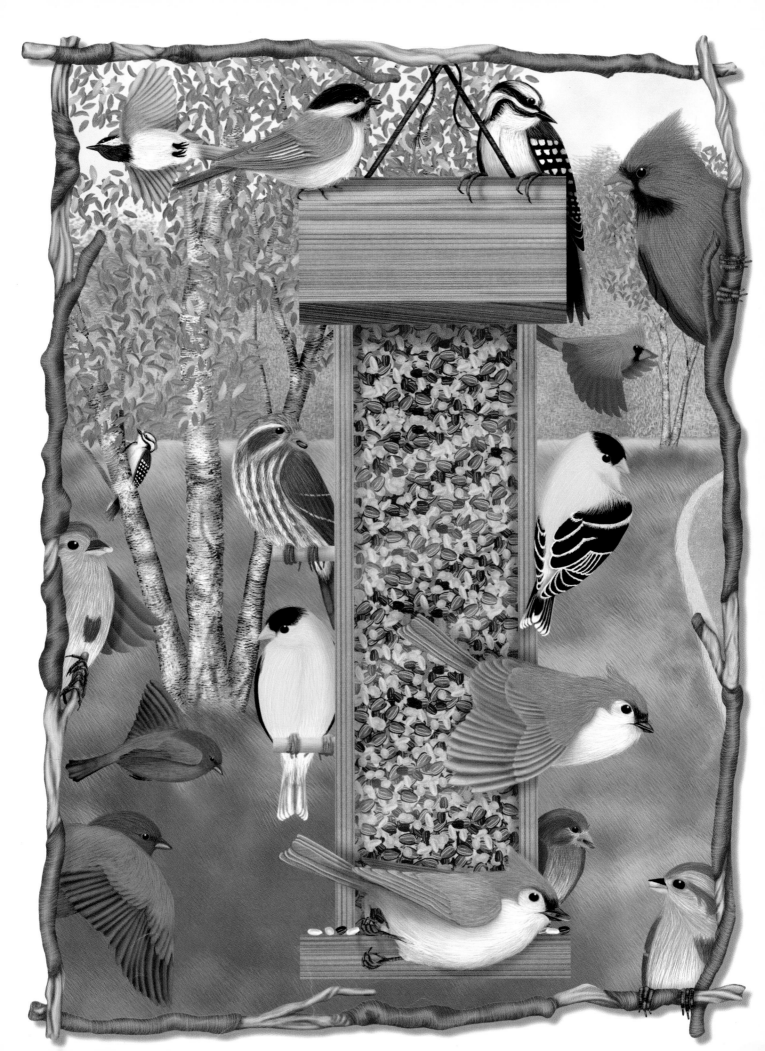

17   18

Seventeen and eighteen
 join this array.
These two nuthatches
 will soon fly away.
For now they relax
 and wait for the chance
To feed on the seeds
 they eye with a glance.

Nuthatches, or upside-down birds, are the only common birds that can walk headfirst down tree trunks. Unlike woodpeckers, the white-breasted nuthatch does not use its tail for support when climbing. By moving one strong foot at a time, the nuthatch can move up and down the tree trunk without falling off.

19

The feeder twists when
a blue jay flies in.
Number **nineteen** enjoys
this swift side spin.
He seems imposing
because of his size.
The others react
with utter surprise.

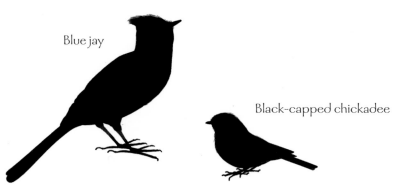

Blue jay

Black-capped chickadee

Blue jays often scare smaller birds at the feeder. Jays are much larger
and need more room to land. Aggressive behavior is common in all birds, but
because the blue jay is twice the size of the smaller birds, its arrival usually
causes a disturbance.

20

The second blue jay,
   the final bird here,
Is looking around
   and showing no fear.
Our count is twenty,
   it's time for the feast.
Twenty is plenty
   for this sneaky beast.

Blue jays eat sunflower seeds from the feeder but prefer acorns. In the fall when acorns are available, blue jays pick off the caps with their beaks and eat the nutmeat they find inside. Like squirrels, blue jays also hide extra acorns for future meals.

Launching himself with
     his prey well in sight,
The cat tries to catch
     the birds in midflight.
But something goes wrong,
     a gray streak lands here,
Scaring his quarry
     that used to be near.

Squirrels are a constant menace to bird feeders. In an attempt to get to the
seeds quicker, squirrels often chew the wood or plastic feeder. One good
way to keep them off your feeder is to hang it eight feet away from branches
and six feet above the ground.

20

One selfish squirrel

 spoiled all the cat's fun.

And as you can see,

 his plan is now done.

The cat feels sad

 because he missed a treat—

Twenty birds are now

 feeding down the street.

It is estimated that over one hundred billion birds live on earth. That means there are more birds than people. We are surrounded by birds! Hang a feeder and birds will come to feed—you can count on it!

A guide to the birds in this book

Black-capped chickadee   1   2

Has a black cap and bib. The male and female look similar.

Tufted titmouse   3   4

A small gray bird with a tufted crest. Both the male and female look alike.

Downy woodpecker   5   6

These birds look similar with the exception of the male's red patch of feathers behind his head.

American goldfinch   7   8

In the summer, the female's feathers are duller than the male's. This difference helps the female blend into the environment, which is important when she is sitting on her nest.

American tree sparrow   9   10

Is identified by a single dark spot on its chest, solid reddish brown cap, gray face and chest, and a beak that is dark on top and yellow on the bottom. Both the male and female look the same.

Northern cardinal   11   12

The male is red and the female is olive brown with red highlights. The female's color helps hide her when she is sitting on her nest. Both have red beaks.

Purple finch   13   14

The male has a raspberry color on his head, back, belly, and rump, and the female is brown and white with brown stripes going down her chest and belly.

Indigo bunting   15   16

The male is a brilliant blue. The female is drab in color. A predator will have difficulty locating her when she is sitting on her nest.

White-breasted nuthatch   17   18

These birds look alike with the exception of the male's black cap.

Blue jay   19   20

A blue bird with a crest, white spots on tail and wings, and a black neck band. The male and female look similar.